Thomas

by Iain Gray

WRITING *to* REMEMBER

79 Main Street, Newtongrange,
Midlothian EH22 4NA
Tel: 0131 344 0414
E-mail: info@lang-syne.co.uk
www.langsyneshop.co.uk

Design by Dorothy Meikle
Printed by Printwell Ltd
© Lang Syne Publishers Ltd 2025

All rights reserved. No part of this publication may be reproduced, stored or introduced into a retrieval system, or transmitted in any form or by any means (electronic, mechanical, photocopying, recording or otherwise) without the prior written permission of Lang Syne Publishers Ltd.

ISBN 978-1-85217-673-0

Thomas

MOTTO:
I Dduw Bo'r Diolch *(Welsh)*
– To God Be Thanks.

CREST:
A Cornish chough.

NAME variations include:
Tomas
Thomasett

Chapter one:

Origins of Welsh surnames

by Iain Gray

If you don't know where you came from, you won't know where you're going **is a frequently quoted observation and one that has a particular resonance today when there has been a marked upsurge in interest in genealogy, with increasing numbers of people curious to trace their family roots.**

Main sources for genealogical research include census returns and official records of births, marriages and deaths – and the key to unlocking the detail they contain is obviously a family surname, one that has been 'inherited' and passed from generation to generation.

No matter our station in life, we all have a surname – but it was not until about the middle of the fourteenth century that the practice of being identified by a particular, or 'fixed', surname became commonly established throughout the British Isles.

Previous to this, it was normal for a person to be identified through the use of only a forename.

Wales, however, known in the Welsh language as *Cymru*, is uniquely different – with the use of what are known as patronymic names continuing well into the fifteenth century and, in remote rural areas, up until the early nineteenth century.

Patronymic names are ones where a son takes his father's forename, or Christian name, as his surname.

Examples of patronymic names throughout the British Isles include 'Johnson', indicating 'son of John', while specifically in Scotland 'son of' was denoted by the prefix Mc or Mac – with 'MacDonald', for example, meaning 'son of Donald.'

Early Welsh law, known as *Cyfraith Hywel*, *The Law of Hywel*, introduced by Hywel the Good, who ruled from Prestatyn to Pembroke between 915 AD and 950 AD, stipulated that a person's name should indicate their ancestry – the name in effect being a type of 'family tree.'

This required the prefixes *ap* or *ab* – derived from *mab*, meaning 'son of' being placed before the person's baptismal name.

In the case of females, the suffixes *verch* or *ferch*, sometimes shortened to *vch* or *vz* would be attached to their Christian name to indicate 'daughter of.'

In some cases, rather than being known for

example as *Llewellyn ap Thomas* – *Llewellyn son of Thomas* – Llewellyn's name would incorporate an 'ancestral tree' going back much earlier than his father.

One source gives the example of *Llewellyn ap Thomas ap Dafydd ap Evan ap Owen ap John* – meaning *Llewellyn son of Thomas son of Dafydd son of Evan son of Owen son of John*.

This leads to great confusion, to say the least, when trying to trace a person's ancestry back to a particular family – with many people having the forenames, for example, of Llewellyn, Thomas, Owen or John.

The first Act of Union between Wales and England that took place in 1536 during the reign of Henry VIII required that all Welsh names be registered in an Anglicised form – with *Hywel*, for example, becoming Howell, or Powell, and *Gruffydd* becoming Griffiths.

An early historical example of this concerns William ap John Thomas, standard bearer to Henry VIII, who became William Jones.

In many cases – as in Davies and Williams – an s was simply added to the original patronymic name, while in other cases the prefix *ap* or *ab* was contracted to *p* or *b* to prefix the name – as in *ab Evan* to form Bevan and *ap Richard* to form Pritchard.

Other original Welsh surnames – such as Morgan, originally *Morcant* – derive from ancient Celtic sources, while others stem from a person's physical characteristics – as in *Gwyn* or *Wynne* a nickname for someone with fair hair, *Gough* or *Gooch* denoting someone with red hair or a ruddy complexion, *Gethin* indicating swarthy or ugly and *Lloyd* someone with brown or grey hair.

With many popular surnames found today in Wales being based on popular Christian names such as John, this means that what is known as the 'stock' or 'pool' of names is comparatively small compared to that of common surnames found in England, Scotland and Ireland.

This explains why, in a typical Welsh village or town with many bearers of a particular name not necessarily being related, they were differentiated by being known, for example, as 'Jones the butcher', 'Jones the teacher' and 'Jones the grocer.'

Another common practice, dating from about the nineteenth century, was to differentiate among families of the same name by prefixing it with the mother's surname or hyphenating the name.

The history of the origins and development of Welsh surnames is inextricably bound up with the nation's frequently turbulent history and its rich culture.

Speaking a Celtic language known as Brythonic, which would gradually evolve into Welsh, the natives were subjected to Roman invasion in 48 AD, and in the following centuries to invasion by the Anglo-Saxons, Vikings and Normans.

Under England's ruthless and ambitious Edward I, the nation was fortified with castles between 1276 and 1295 to keep the 'rebellious' natives in check – but this did not prevent a series of bloody uprisings against English rule that included, most notably, Owain Glyndŵr's rebellion in 1400.

Politically united with England through the first Act of Union in 1536, becoming part of the Kingdom of Great Britain in 1707 and part of the United Kingdom in 1801, it was in 1999 that *Cynulliad Cenedlaethol Cymru*, the National Assembly for Wales, was officially opened by the Queen.

Welsh language and literature has flourished throughout the nation's long history.

In what is known as the Heroic Age, early Welsh poets include the late sixth century Taliesin and Aneirin, author of *Y Gododdin*.

Discovered in a thirteenth century manuscript but thought to date from anywhere between the seventh and eleventh centuries, it refers to the kingdom of Gododdin that took in south-east Scotland and

Northumberland and was part of what was once the Welsh territory known as *Hen Ogledd, The Old North*.

Commemorating Gododdin warriors who were killed in battle against the Angles of Bernicia and Deira at Catraith in about 600 AD, the manuscript – known as *Llyfr Aneirin, Book of Aneirin* – is now in the precious care of Cardiff City Library.

Other important early works by Welsh poets include the fourteenth century *Red Book of Hergest*, now held in the Bodleian Library, Oxford, and the *White Book of Rhydderch*, kept in the National Library of Wales, Aberystwyth.

William Morgan's translation of the Bible into Welsh in 1588 is hailed as having played an important role in the advancement of the Welsh language, while in 1885 Dan Isaac Davies founded the first Welsh language society.

It was in 1856 that Evan James and his son James James composed the rousing Welsh national anthem *Hen Wlad Fynhadad – Land of My Fathers*, while in the twentieth century the poet Dylan Thomas gained international fame and acclaim with poems such as *Under Milk Wood*.

The nation's proud cultural heritage is also celebrated through *Eisteddfod Genedlaethol Cymru*, the National Eisteddfod of Wales, the annual festival of music, literature and performance that is held across the nation and which traces its roots back to 1176 when Rhys ap Gruffyd, who ruled the territory of Deheubarth from 1155 to 1197, hosted a magnificent festival of poetry and song at his court in Cardigan.

The 2011 census for Wales unfortunately shows that the number of people able to speak the language has declined from 20.8% of the population of just under 3.1 million in 2001 to 19% – but overall the nation's proud culture, reflected in its surnames, still flourishes.

Many Welsh families proudly boast the heraldic device known as a Coat of Arms, as featured on our front cover.

The central motif of the Coat of Arms would originally have been what was borne on the shield of a warrior to distinguish himself from others on the battlefield.

Not featured on the Coat of Arms, but highlighted on page three, is the family motto and related crest – with the latter frequently different from the central motif.

Echoes of a far distant past can still be found in our surnames and they can be borne with pride in commemoration of our forebears.

Chapter two:

Invasion and conquest

Of truly Biblical roots, 'Thomas' derives from an ancient Aramaic word meaning 'twin', and as a forename it was popularised through reverence for the apostle Thomas, known as 'doubting Thomas', because he at first doubted the truth of Christ's resurrection.

Finally convinced, he went on to fervently preach Christ's message throughout the Middle East and even much further afield – and is believed to have been martyred in India.

The name was also popularised in the Christian tradition through reverence for the twelfth century Archbishop of Canterbury and martyr St Thomas Becket, and for the thirteenth century Italian theologian St Thomas Aquinas, while as a surname it indicates 'son of Thomas.'

In Wales, the early heartland of those who would come to bear the Thomas name was the ancient kingdom of Brycheiniog – now modern-day Breconshire.

One of the nation's thirteen historic counties it is also known as Brecknockshire, County of Brecon,

County of Brecknock and, in Welsh, as *Sir Frycheiniog* – with 'Sir' denoting 'County'.

The first serious threat to the kingdom's independence came in the sixth century in the form of the Anglo-Saxons – those Germanic tribes who invaded and settled in the south and east of the island of Britain from about the early fifth century.

Composed of the Jutes, from the area of the Jutland Peninsula in modern Denmark, the Saxons from Lower Saxony and the Angles from the Angeln area of Germany, it was the latter who gave the name 'Engla land', or 'Aengla land' – better known as 'England.'

The Anglo-Saxons meanwhile, had usurped the power of the indigenous Britons, who referred to them as 'Saeson' or 'Saxones' – and it is from this that the Welsh term for English people of 'Saeson' derives, the Scottish-Gaelic 'Sasannach' and the Irish-Gaelic 'Sasanach.'

We learn from the *Anglo-Saxon Chronicle* how the religion of the early Anglo-Saxons was one that pre-dated the establishment of Christianity in the British Isles by about 690 A.D.

But, as a form of Germanic paganism with roots in Old Norse religion, it shared much in common with the Druidic 'nature-worshipping' religion of the indigenous Britons such as the Welsh.

The death knell of Anglo-Saxon supremacy was sounded with the Norman Conquest of 1066 when Harold II was defeated at the battle of Hastings, in East Sussex, by a mighty invasion force led by Duke William II of Normandy.

William was declared King of England on December 25, and the complete subjugation of his Anglo-Saxon subjects followed, with those Normans who had fought on his behalf rewarded with lands – a pattern that would be followed in Wales.

Invading across the Welsh Marches, the borderland between England and Wales, the Normans gradually consolidated their gains – with ancient Welsh kingdoms such as the early Thomas heartland of Brycheiniog being taken over by them as 'Lordships'.

Under a succession of Welsh leaders who included Llywelyn ap Gruffudd, known as Llywelyn the Last, resistance proved strong.

But Llwelyn's resistance was brutally crushed in 1283 under England's ruthless and ambitious Edward I, who ordered the building or repair of at least 17 castles and in 1302 proclaimed his son and heir, the future Edward II, as Prince of Wales, a title known in Welsh as *Tywysog Cymru*.

Another heroic Welsh figure dominated the resistance movement from 1400 to 1415 in the form of

Owain Glyndŵr – the last native Welshman to be recognised by his supporters as *Tywysog Cymru*, and it is from this charismatic freedom fighter that some bearers of the Thomas name today claim a proud descent.

In what is known as The Welsh Revolt he achieved an early series of stunning victories against Henry IV and his successor Henry V – until mysteriously disappearing from the historical record after mounting an ambush in Brecon.

Some sources assert that he was either killed in the ambush or died a short time afterwards from wounds he received – but there is a persistent tradition that he survived and lived thereafter in anonymity, protected by loyal followers.

During the revolt, he had consistently refused offers of a Royal Pardon and – despite offers of hefty rewards for his capture – he was never betrayed.

One noted fifteenth century bearer of the Thomas name was William ap Thomas, an ancestor of the Earls of Pembroke through his son William Herbert, 1st Earl of Pembroke.

Responsible for expanding the forbidding edifice that is Raglan Castle, in Monmouthshire, he fought on many campaigns on behalf of the English Crown, most notably beside Henry V at the battle of

Agincourt in October of 1415, during The Hundred Years War, when a great victory was achieved over the French.

Knighted in 1426 by Henry's successor, Henry VI, and known in Welsh as *Y Marchog Glas o Went* – The Blue Knight of Gwent – because of the colour of his armour, his second wife was the heiress Gwladys ferch Dafydd, described poetically as 'The Star of Abergavenny' because of her beauty.

William ap Thomas died in 1445 and Gwladys in 1454 and both were buried in Abergavenny Priory, of which they were patrons.

It was their son William, born in 1423 and who died in 1469, who was created 1st Earl of Pembroke after having adopted 'Herbert' as his surname.

Chapter three:

Business and politics

Bearers of the Thomas name have also achieved historical fame as entrepreneurs and politicians.

Recognised as having not only revolutionised the iron industry in his native Wales but also influential in the birth of the industrial revolution in the United States, David Thomas was born in 1794 in Cadoxton, near Neath.

The son of a farmer, he turned his back on the land for a much different career in the smoke and din of the iron industry, finding employment in the Swansea Valley at the Yniscedwyn Works, in Ystradgynlais.

It was in 1837 that, using a hot blast technique to smelt anthracite coal and iron ore, he developed a simple method to produce anthracite iron.

Recognised by this date as one of Britain's leading ironmasters, he took up employment two years later with the Lehigh Coal and Navigation Company in Lehigh County, Pennsylvania – building a furnace for the production of anthracite iron.

This proved a success and, two years later and along with his son Samuel, he set up his own ironworks in the small Pennsylvanian community of Catasauqua –

and it was the iron produced from this works that built the first American-made cast-iron construction columns, pipes and tunnel tubes.

This included iron used in the construction of New York City's Lincoln and Holland Tunnels.

A noted philanthropist and with he and his wife Elizabeth known as "the father and mother of Catasauqua", a founder of the American Association of Industrial Engineers and the first president of the American Society of Metallurgy, he died in 1882.

Not only a prominent Welsh industrialist but also a Liberal Party politician, David Alfred Thomas, better known as D.A. Thomas and later more formally as 1st Viscount Rhondda, was born in 1856.

The son of the coalmine owner Samuel Thomas, of Ysguborwen, Aberdare, he eventually took over control of the family business of Cambrian Collieries and greatly expanded it.

A frequently controversial figure, he refused to take the side of fellow members of what was known as the Cambrian Combine during a strike by miners in 1898, and subsequently stated he felt 'betrayed' when his employees were involved in a strike two years later.

This strike culminated in the infamous Tonypandy Riots, also known as the Rhondda Riots, when the then Home Secretary Winston Churchill controversially despatched troops to South Wales to break the strikers' resolve – still a cause of resentment to this day.

Owner of Llanwern House, near Newport, Monmouthshire, Thomas served as Liberal Party Member of Parliament (MP) for Merthyr Tydfil from 1888 until 1910 and then for Cardiff.

Having served for a time during the First World War as Minister for Food Control and as Prime Minister David Lloyd George's special emissary to the United States, he died in 1918, only a short time after being created Viscount Rhondda.

One particularly colourful and feisty bearer of the Thomas name was his daughter Margaret Haig Thomas – the author, newspaper editor and campaigner for women's rights who took the title of Viscountess Rhondda following her father's death.

Born in 1883 in Bayswater, London, and educated at St Leonard's School in the Scottish east coast town of St Andrews – where her mother's family, the Haigs, hailed from – and for a brief period at Somerville College, Oxford, she settled in Wales and worked for a time as her father's business secretary.

Marrying Humphrey Mackworth in 1908, with Mackworth inheriting his father's baronetcy six years later, she settled in Llansoar, Monmouthshire, but the couple became estranged – not least because she was a Liberal and he was a Conservative.

Ignoring her husband's protests, she became actively involved in the suffragette campaign for women's rights that included the right to vote.

A member of the Women's Social and Political Union, one of her exploits involved jumping onto the running-board of Prime Minister H.H. Asquith's car while he was visiting St Andrews, while she also learned how to set pillar boxes alight as a form of protest.

Sentenced to a month's imprisonment for her actions on behalf of the suffragist cause in Gwent, she stubbornly refused to eat and was released after spending ten days behind bars.

With the suffragettes rallying behind the national interest during the dark days of the First World War of 1914 to 1918, in the final year of the conflict the government entrusted her with the post of 'chief recruiting officer' for women in Britain – encouraging them to aid the war effort.

Three years earlier, in May of 1915, both she and her father were among the survivors when the German submarine *U-20* torpedoed and sank the transatlantic cruise liner *Lusitania* off the south coast of Ireland – with the loss of 1,200 lives.

At the end of the war, and along with a group of other women, she founded the politically independent weekly newspaper *Time and Tide*, editing it for nearly 40 years.

Having divorced her husband in 1923 and with the couple not having had any children, her family's title became extinct on her death in 1958.

One bearer of the Thomas name who came to hold high government office, Thomas George Thomas was the British Labour Party politician more formally known as 1st Viscount Tonypandy.

Born in 1909 in Port Talbot, the son of a miner, he was employed for a time as a schoolteacher before being elected MP for Cardiff Central in 1945.

Holding this seat until 1950, he then held the seat of Cardiff West until his retirement from the House of Commons in 1983.

During the administration of Prime Minister Harold Wilson, he had held the post from 1968 to 1970 as Secretary of State for Wales, while from 1976 to 1983 he was Speaker of the House of Commons.

Raised to the Peerage as Viscount Tonypandy of Rhondda, in the County of Mid Glamorgan, it was seven years after his death in 1997 that the former Welsh Labour MP Leo Abse controversially claimed in his book *Tony Blair: The Man Behind the Smile*, that the former Speaker had been the victim of blackmail because of his alleged homosexuality.

In contemporary politics, Dafydd Elis Elis-Thomas, more formally known as Baron Elis-Thomas, is the Welsh politician born in Carmarthen in 1946 and who was raised in the Llandysul area of Ceredigion and in Llanrwst, in the Conwy Valley.

Having served as a Plaid Cymru MP for Merionnydd and for Meirionnydd Nant Conwy and a former leader of his party, he held the position of Presiding Officer of the National Assembly for Wales from its inception in 1999 until 2011.

Chapter four:

On the world stage

In the great Welsh literary tradition, Dylan Thomas was the poet and writer born Dylan Marlais Thomas in Swansea in 1914.

Acknowledged as one of the most important Welsh poets of the twentieth century, he worked for a short period as a journalist after leaving school when aged 16.

Aged only 20 when his poem *Light breaks where no sun shines* caught the attention of the literary world, he rose to international acclaim with a number of other noted works that include *Fern Hill*, *Under Milk Wood*, *Do not go gentle into that good night* and *Death shall have no dominion*.

Embarking on a series of reading tours and radio broadcasts he soon acquired a reputation, in his own words, as a "roistering, drunken and doomed poet."

Along with his wife Caitlin Macnamara, Thomas did indeed have an unfortunate relationship with alcohol, dying after a drunken binge in November of 1953 while visiting New York.

Shortly after their marriage, the couple had settled in Laugharne, Carmarthenshire and their home, known as The Boathouse, is now the Dylan Thomas Museum.

The poet is also honoured in his birthplace of Swansea with the Dylan Thomas Theatre and a bronze statue that stands outside the literary venue the Dylan Thomas Centre.

Another memorial to him is a small rock that stands in one of his favourite childhood haunts of Swansea's Cwmdonkin Park.

Inscribed on the rock are the poignant closing lines of *Fern Hill*:

> *Oh as I was young and easy*
> *in the mercy of his means*
> *Time held me green and dying*
> *Though I sang in my chains like the sea*

Bearers of the Thomas name have also gained acclaim in the world of film.

Characterised by his distinctive voice, a prominent gap between his two upper front teeth and props and costume that included a monocle, large cigarette holder and waistcoat, Thomas Terry Hoar Stevens was the English comic actor better known by his stage name of **Terry-Thomas**.

Born in 1911 in Finchley, London, he rose from performing in amateur dramatics, vaudeville and, during the Second World, with ENSA (Entertainments National

Service Association) to international fame through his roles in a number of films.

Playing the role of a 'cad' or 'bounder', speaking in an upper-middle class accent, these films include the 1957 *Blue Murder at St. Trinian's*, the 1959 *I'm All Right Jack*, the 1959 *Carlton-Browne of the F.O.*, the 1963 *It's A Mad, Mad, Mad, Mad World* and, from 1965, *Those Magnificent Men In Their Flying Machines*.

Also renowned for having written and starring in the 1949 *How Do You View*, the first comedy series on British television, he died in 1990 as a result of the degenerative Parkinson's disease.

Having spent most of the money he had earned from his film career in an attempt to battle the disease, he died in poverty – with his final years, through support from the Actors' Benevolent Charity, spent in a nursing home.

One of an American acting 'dynasty', **Danny Thomas** starred in films that include the 1951 *I'll See You in My Dreams*, with Doris Day and, with the singer Peggy Lee, the 1952 remake of *The Jazz Singer*.

Born Amos Yakhoob Kairoul in Detroit in 1912, the son of Lebanese immigrants to America, the nightclub comedian, film and television actor and producer was also known for his own sitcom, *Make*

Room for Daddy, while he produced television shows that most notably included *The Dick Van Dyke Show*.

Earlier in his career, as what he described as a "starving actor", he vowed that if he ever achieved success he would dedicate a shrine to St Jude Thaddeus – the patron saint of hopeless causes.

He fulfilled this vow in 1962 when, along with others, he founded what today is the centre of medical excellence known as the St Jude Children's Hospital, in Memphis.

Dedicated to treating and finding cures for sick children from not only throughout the United States but also further afield, the hospital's Dr Peter C. Doherty was the recipient in 1996 of the Nobel Prize In Physiology or Medicine for discoveries on how the immune system works to kill cells infected by viruses.

An inductee of the Television Hall of Fame he died in 1991, while in 2012 the United States Postal Service issued a stamp honouring him as both an entertainer and as a humanitarian.

Closely involved in promoting the work of the hospital founded by her father, Margaret Julia Thomas is the award-winning actress, producer and social activist better known as **Marlo Thomas**, born in 1937 and best known for her role from 1966 to 1971 in the sitcom *That*

Girl and for the children's television series *Free to Be... You and Me*.

The recipient of a Grammy Award, four Emmy Awards and, in 2014, the Presidential Medal of Freedom, she is also the recipient of a Women in Film Lucy Award for her "excellence and innovation in her creative works that have enhanced the perception of women through the medium of television".

She is the sister, meanwhile, of the film and television producer Charles Anthony Thomas, better known as **Tony Thomas**.

Born in 1948, he is known for his production work on films that include the 1989 *Dead Poets Society* and television series that include *Benson* and *The Golden Girls*, while **Philip Michael Thomas**, born in 1949, is the American actor who first rose to fame in the role of Detective Richard Tubbs in the 1980s' television series *Miami Vice*.

Known for her role of Lucy Bates in the television police drama series *Hill Street Blues*, **Betty Thomas** is the married name of the actress and film and television director born Betty Lucille Nienhauser in St Louis, Missouri, in 1948.

Her directing credits include *Hooperman*, the 1995 *The Brady Bunch Movie* and, from 2009, *Alvin and the Chipmunks: The Squeakquel*.

Born in 1980, **Eddie Kaye Thomas** is the American actor known for his role of Paul Finch in the *American Pie* series of comedy films, while on British shores **Gareth Thomas** is the Welsh actor best known for his role of Roj Blake in the *Blake's 7* television series.

Born in 1945, his many other television credits include *The Avengers*, *Casualty*, *Midsomer Murders* and *Torchwood*.

With television credits that include the role of Tom Henshall in *Cutting It* and of Charles Quance in the serial *The House of Eliott*, **Bill Thomas** is the actor of both stage and screen born in London in 1952, while also on the television screen **Ryan Thomas**, born in 1984, is the English actor known for his role of Jason Grimshaw in the soap *Coronation Street*.

Behind the camera lens, **Jeremy Thomas** is the award-winning British producer born in Hull in 1949; the recipient of a CBE, he produced the 1988 *The Last Emperor*, winner of the Academy Award for Best Picture.

Born in India to English parents in 1940, **Antony Thomas** is the acclaimed documentary filmmaker whose award-winning work includes the controversial 1980 drama-documentary *Death of a Princess*, based on what is purported to be the true story of a young Saudi Arabian princess and her lover who were publicly executed for adultery.

From the stage to music, **Ray Thomas** is the English singer, flautist and composer with the band The Moody Blues.

Born in 1941, his many compositions for the band include *Legend of a Mind*, *Dear Diary* and *Nice to Be Here*.

An inductee of the Rock and Roll Hall of Fame, **Charlie Thomas** is the American rhythm and blues singer born in 1937 in Lynchburg, Virginia who is best known as a member of the band The Drifters whose international hits include *When My Little Girl Is Smiling* and *Sweets For My Sweet*.

An inductee of the Canadian Music Hall of Fame, David Henry Thomsett is the musician, singer and songwriter better known as **David Clayton-Thomas**.

Born in Surrey in 1941, the son of a Canadian soldier then stationed in England and later moving with his family to Canada, he is best known as a member of the band Blood Sweat & Tears, whose hits include *Spinning Wheel* and *You Made Me So Very Happy*.

In a different musical genre, **Mansel Thomas** was the Welsh composer and conductor who from 1950 until 1965 was BBC Wales Head of Music.

Born in 1909 in Pontygwaith, near Tylorstown, Rhondda, it was through a Rhondda Scholarship that he was able, at the age of only 16, to study at the Royal Academy of Music in London.

Later principal conductor for a time of the BBC Welsh Orchestra and the composer of a number of works that included solo vocal, choral, instrumental, band and orchestral, he died in 1986.

The recipient of an OBE for his services to music, other honours bestowed on him in his lifetime include the John Edwards Memorial Award by The Guild for the Promotion of Welsh Music.

Bearers of the Thomas name have also excelled in the highly competitive world of sport.

Born in 1890 in Bettws, Bridgend, **Horace Thomas** was the Welsh international rugby union fly-half who was also a talented cricketer and athlete.

Having played club rugby for Swansea and the recipient of two caps, he was one of thirteen Welsh internationals to be killed in action during the First World War.

The recipient of 27 caps for his country, **Malcolm Thomas** was the Welsh and British Lions rugby union player born in Machen in 1929; having played club rugby for Newport, he died in 2012.

Nicknamed "Alfie", **Gareth Thomas** is, at the

time of writing, the second highest try scorer for Wales, behind Shane Williams.

Born in 1974 and having represented his nation in both rugby union and rugby league, it was in 2009 that he became the first openly gay professional rugby union player after announcing his sexuality and stating: "I don't want to be known as a gay rugby player.

"I am a rugby player, first and foremost I am a man."

From rugby to the cycling track, **Geraint Thomas**, born in 1986 in Whitchurch, Cardiff is the Welsh professional rider whose many successes include winning the 2010 British National Road Race Championships and also an Olympic gold medal for the team pursuit.

Welsh bearers of the Thomas name have also achieved fame in the boxing ring.

Born in Merthyr Tydfil in 1926, **Eddie Thomas** held the titles of Welsh welterweight champion, British and European Champion and the British Empire title.

The recipient of an MBE and at one time mayor of Merthyr Tydfil, he died in 1997.

Born in 1880 at Carnceyn Farm, Pen-y-graig, Glamorganshire, **Thomas Thomas** was Britain's first middle-weight boxing champion – achieving this two years before his death in 1911 from acute rheumatism.

On the athletics track, **Iwan Thomas** is the sprinter born in Farnborough, London in 1974.

The recipient of an MBE, he is now a television celebrity, having appeared on programmes that include *Through the Keyhole*, *Celebrity Master Chef* and *The Wright Stuff*.

On the golf course, **David Thomas**, born in 1934, was not only a Welsh professional player but also a noted golf course architect.

Having represented Britain in the Ryder Cup in 1959, 1963, 1965 and 1967, he died in 2013 – while golf courses he designed include The Belfry, in Warwickshire.

On an artistic note, Herbert Samuel Thomas, better known as **Bert Thomas**, was the political cartoonist and contributor to the humourist magazine *Punch* born in 1883 in Rodney Wharf, Newport, Monmouthshire.

Known for his popular First World War propaganda cartoon "Arf a mo, Kaiser" and his Second World War "Arf a mo, 'Itler" and the recipient of an MBE, he died in 1966.